Business Strategies
in Times of Crisis

Business Strategies in Times of Crisis

Dr. Charles O. Usigbe

Rev. date: 12/04/2015

To order additional copies of this book, contact:
Xlibris
1-888-795-4274
www.Xlibris.com
Orders@Xlibris.com
730498

CONTENTS

CONTENTS

ACKNOWLEDGEMENTS

I AM GRATEFUL for several kinds of aid, without which this book could not have been completed so, I would like to express my sincere appreciation to those people who helped me in the completion of my book.

I would like to thank my brothers and sister both in US, South Africa and Nigeria. Sister Agness Uzeh, Mr. Matthew Usigbe Mrs. Grace E. Usigbe, Mrs. Caroline Ugbodu, Pastor Solomon Ugbodu, Mr. & Mrs. Chris Usigbe, Mr. & Mrs. Morris Usigbe, Mrs. Franca Iyere, & Mr. Thompson Iyere Mrs. Debra Adepoju, & Mr. Adepoju, Mrs. Nance Chukwu Emeka, Mrs. Rose Okoduwa & all my Nephews and Nieces. They are always there for me, both good times and bad times thanks to all of you. Also thanks to Princes Joan Okojie for the moral support. Special thanks to my father Chief Jeremiah Okokoni Usigbe with his continue prayers for me I Prevail. Also thanks to my office secretary Annette Mattox for all her support with the office work, this makes it easy for me to study. The person who made all of this possible is my wife Melissa Usigbe. Her constant support and care aided me throughout the study. Thanks to Melissa Usigbe. The typing and editing burden was borne by Mr. Mark kabtown thanks to Mr. Mark for his support.

CHAPTER 1

Introduction

Problem Statement

The problem facing many businesses today is being able to conduct business during times of crisis. Businesses must walk with extreme caution during times of crisis and be extremely sensitive to the issues at hand. A crisis represents "a low probability, high impact situation that is perceived by critical stakeholders to threaten the viability of the organization" (Pearson and Clair 2008, p. 66).

Purpose of the Study

The purpose of the study is to examine business strategies during times of crises. Over the past several years the United States has had several tragic events occur in the form of terrorism and natural disasters. The travesties of Hurricane sandy, Hurricane Katrina and the terrorist attack that occurred Sept. 11th 2001 certainly helped us to reflect on the issue of how business must incorporate effective strategies during times of crisis. From a strategic business perspective the cost of the September 11th attacks is staggering, and affects hundreds of related and non-related industries, employees and management of related and non-related companies, and had the effect of stopping an already ailing economy short. Some experts believe the economic damage from

Hurricane sandy, Hurricane Katrina and 9/11 ultimately exceed $245 billion. The stock market, which was already seesawing, has become even more volatile, and hundreds of thousands of blue-collar and white-collar workers have been pink-slipped as the airline, insurance, and securities industries took direct hits. Consumer confidence, at its lowest point since the Persian Gulf War, caused the engine of the economy--spending--to sputter. Never before has the growing interdependence of companies and people been so dramatically illustrated.

It's not an issue of which executives are unaware, although it's one they might wish they could ignore. In his book, *Crisis Management,* Steven Fink's study of Fortune 500 CEOs indicated that they all felt they were at least partially exposed and/or vulnerable to the following kinds of crisis: industrial accidents; environmental problems: union problems/strikes; product recalls; investor relations; hostile takeovers; proxy fights; rumors/media leaks; government regulatory problems; acts of terrorism; and embezzlement.

Importance of the Study

Highly visible disasters such as terrorist attacks and natural disasters focus the attention of the public and the business community on the vulnerability of companies, their profitability and maintenance of ongoing operations; to that end, companies develop contingency strategies in the form of disaster recovery plans. A function of risk management, disaster recovery plans are designed to enable a company to return to business as usual as soon as possible.

The traditional definition of management includes the 'planning, implementation and control' of activities and events in various areas of responsibility. Professional managers cannot leave events to chance; a crisis may affect any or all areas of management functions including but not limited to: accounting, finance, risk marketing and human resources. The management of a crisis, therefore, is just as much a part of management responsibilities as are the more traditional, 'business as usual' functions in normal times.

Disaster recovery and crisis management planning and strategies target operations and functions within a company to ensure operational continuance and return to profitability, but for the most part tend to ignore the impact interruption of business may have to the constituents to whom the company may have a responsibility.

However, just as individuals interact, so companies in the business world are interconnect and interact. A very high profile example of this is the recent terrorist attack on the World Trade Center. Overall, very few of the businesses in the world were affected; only a miniscule percentage of the world's population; only one city in tens of thousands of cities worldwide. The attack was perpetrated by less than 50 people – and yet the effect is felt far beyond those immediately involved, through a business phenomenon that can be called the "ripple" or "multiplier effect". The "multiplier effect" is typically used to explain how the value of a dollar spent at one business "multiplies" as it effects several different types of goods and services and "ripples" outward into the economy. Consequently, the attack affected the companies involved, insurance companies, airlines, tourism, state income tax collected, Wall Street prices and world stock exchanges and economies.

Similarly, a company has certain contacts and constituents in the course of doing business, developing, contributing to, and exploiting a web of mutually beneficial interaction. Due to the fact that they have a written or implied symbiotic agreement of commerce which they encouraged as part of doing business, and the relationships they built through trust (employer/employee, supplier/customer, company/investor, etc), they have an ethical responsibility to anticipate the effects a disaster or slowdown for their business would have on these entities or individuals and to make provisions. They do this by means of a disaster recovery plan, written prior to an accident or crisis.

Scope of the Study

Responsible crisis planning and strategies is a learning process in which organizations learn from thoughtful evaluation of all aspects of their environment, including customers, suppliers and competitors, and take both short-and long-term organizational goals into consideration (Kohli and Jaworski 2010). However, because crises are unique, low-probability situations, firms do not encounter them frequently and therefore cannot learn about them in advance. Also, learning from non-unique crisis situations is less likely to prove useful because firms rarely encounter these situations, do not have ample opportunity to use their learning about crises, and therefore would be less motivated to learn and prepare.

Crises "defy interpretations and impose severe demands on sensemaking" (Weick 2013, p. 305). It is possible that even an organizational capability as pervasive as risk management may not be anticipate the rare circumstances that organizations can face in a crisis. Highly attuned internal and external orientation would cause firms to lock into a standard mode of cognition and response, providing a planned, reasoned reaction – combined with knowledge of the organization and environment, multi-factored decision making can be effectively made.

In times of crisis, the appropriate form of strategic flexibility is reactive. Because the extent, nature, and timing of a crisis are difficult to predict, proactive offensive action to manage the crisis is unlikely, so reactive strategic flexibility capability is useful. Organizations develop reactive strategic flexibility (henceforth, we use the term "strategic flexibility" to refer to "reactive strategic flexibility") by building excess and liquid resources (Cyert and March 1963) and creating the capacity to be agile and versatile. To achieve agility and versatility, organizations instill capabilities for responding to diverse scenarios. Such capabilities are built by placing emphasis on the management of environmental diversity and variability (Evans 2011).

When the benefits of adapting outweigh the gains from standardized strategy, as in crisis situations, strategic flexibility capabilities are likely to be useful. The exact meaning and conceptualization of strategic flexibility varies from one context to another: typically, strategic flexibility represents the organizational ability to manage economic and political risks by promptly responding in a proactive or reactive manner to threats (and opportunities), thereby making it possible for firms to resort to what Ansoff (2012) terms "surprise management." Strategic flexibility is expected to increase the effectiveness of communications, plans, and strategies, which should enhance firm performance and resiliency in the face of crisis.

A crisis represents an anomaly and has the potential to change the very basis of how a firm does business. Firms that have the flexibility to respond to the new environment altered by the conditions of crisis and "rise to the occasion" are at a definite advantage; they can easily redeploy critical resources and mobilize the diversity of strategic options available to them to maximize the probability of corporate survival, while ensuring viability of the supply lines and customer base vital for long term, 'down-the-road profitability.

Rationale of the Study

Strategic flexibility, by definition, emphasizes answering the unique needs of consumers, business partners, and institutional constituents (Allen and Pantzalis 2013). With effective and successful implementation of an ethical recovery plan addressing the interests of constituents, an organizations stands to emerge from the crisis in a stronger position than before – with enhanced loyalty and commitment from constituents for which it has demonstrated concern and perhaps even compassion and empathy. It would follow that the positive relationship between exercising strategic flexibility and ethical firm performance during and after crisis should strengthen and reinforce the web of interrelationships, resulting in increased potential for profitable business partnerships. In conditions of low competitive intensity, investments in flexible resources and strategic options may not be the optimal capital investment, as an organization is less likely to face circumstances that require the use of these resources, and would be under less pressure to perform ethically under the risk of losing clients. However, in highly competitive environments, strategic flexibility is a valuable asset (Aaker and Mascarenhas 2014).

A disaster recovery strategic plan is a comprehensive statement of consistent actions to be taken before, during and after a disaster. The plan should be documented and tested to ensure the continuity of operations and availability of critical resources in the event of a disaster. It is developed by a planning committee of a company or firm; the planning committee should prepare a risk analysis and business impact analysis that includes a range of possible disasters, including natural, technical and human threats and how they will be handled during time of crisis.

Companies nationwide that had the foresight to make and implement a strategic disaster recovery plan sighed and realized a confirmation of their efforts different occasions such as during Hurricane Sandy,

Hurricane Katrina and September 1, 2001. Companies that had either failed to plan or had ignored the advice of risk managers and insurance agents scrambled to come up with one. The employees, suppliers, stockholders and other constituents depending on the ongoing business of the former were comforted in the foresight of their managers in making contingency plans to ensure their interest in uninterrupted operations; the constituents of the latter may have realized with a shock the high level of risk they personally had been exposed to without such plans.

Effective business strategies require that disaster recovery plans take all constituents affected into consideration. The practice of business ethics is an important strategy to maintain during times of crisis. *Ethics* is an inter-relational discipline – if there was only one person on the planet, s/he could be supremely self-centered and totally selfish without social ramifications because society, by definition, would not exist. The "rules" by which interaction takes place assumes a fair and reasonable standard, which will be the basis for our discussion of business ethics in times of crisis.

If a business simply addressed its own concerns in maintaining or resuming operations and profitability, ignoring those affected constituents, it would be neglecting the responsibilities comprising the reciprocal side of the benefits it received from those associations. Most disaster recovery plans do not address these issues, except from the aspect of risk management, when in fact they are marketing and ethical issues as well.

Overview of the Study

Planning is the first step and goes hand in hand with security. The world has seen many crisis situations over the years and terrorism is not a new threat, it just seems to be hitting home right now. Although we have armed and trained security persons on patrol at all times, each employee becomes a security officer in a special way: each employee is (or should be) completely aware of what is normal for their particular area of the plant. Each employee should be alert to changes or irregularities and report them to management and/or security right away. A loose package, suspicious and unusual powder or substance, something not where it should be or a situation or setup that looks "odd" or "funny" can be much more than a coincidence.

It is more important than ever those employees know who and what belongs here and what doesn't. Is that a lunch bag that was left behind in the hallway, a package of documents left on the desk waiting for the secretary to come back from her break, or a bomb? Could that powder be coffee creamer or a dangerous substance placed there to harm or disable our employees? There has been a lot of coverage of "scares" and "hoaxes" and some of them seem silly – point is: they are silly and stupid until just one is real. We need to maintain an attitude of awareness to ethically watch out for ourselves and fellow employees, and yet refrain from cultivating an atmosphere of undue fear and suspicion. This is a risk management problems and involves larger issues of awareness training, open communication and empowered trust and credibility of staff.

Dealing with the conflicting issues of making people feel secure while maintaining vigilance will be a challenge facing all risk management professionals now and in the foreseeable future. Never before has it been so true that if management fails to plan, they're planning to fail.

The purpose of this report is to review traditional loss management and disaster recovery programs and procedures, identify business and human considerations necessary to address to ensure complete and ethical handling of crisis situations and their aftermath on a holistic basis, and provide/propose integrated solutions of human, business and operational issues.

Through the contents of this report we will develop a means by which businesses may consider and completely address operational, ethical, profitability and constituent aspects in planning how to recover from a disaster or crisis that interrupts or impedes normal commerce. Too often businesses focus on the bottom line and lose sight of the people and symbiotic associate aspects that must come together to return the entire business environment to its original health.

Current trends in business include recognition of a firm's place as a part of an interconnecting social and business web: events such as a disaster affecting the firm have a ripple effect extending to shareholders, employees, suppliers and consumers. During times of crisis, a firm must ethically provide for support of those constituents with whom it has encouraged a symbiotic relationship.

Therefore, a business has an ethical responsibility to address constituent concerns, which may be operational, economic, psychological or otherwise, constituents in a responsible disaster recovery plans. This should all be a part of the strategic planning process.

The first objective is to review the existing body of knowledge about the ways businesses are expected to operate with ethical and socially responsible sensitivities, and about how different writers and researchers have analyzed the problems with coping with balancing "doing well" with "doing good" while pursuing the main objective of business continuity.

This report will deal with the diverse considerations, factors and underlying assumptions of doing so, from a premise that business is a social structure and therefore subject to critical review from an ethical, as well as operational standpoint. Research on ethical orientation and strategic flexibility has concentrated on the normal course of a firm's business and as a result has ignored the constructs' impact on the firm's ability to manage crises. Because of increasing globalization and the emergence of the network economy (Achrol and Kotler 2009), sooner or later major crises have a direct or indirect effect on almost every firm. Thus, it is essential to develop an understanding of organizational capabilities that will help firms ethically manage a crisis and its wider impact.

The second objective is to review actual procedures of companies faced with crisis situations and how they handled their diverse constituencies in order to provide examples and conclusions of reasonable, responsible and ethical planning for future risk management and crisis management needs.

A comparative study can provide helpful information to policy-makers seeking improvements in their own approaches to risk management. It is intended that this paper be published to the business community and to risk management professionals to raise awareness of these critical relationships and the need to address a crisis on a holistic basis.

CHAPTER 2

Literature Review

Organizations frequently must cope with anomalous events, referred to as crises, which create high levels of uncertainty and are potential threats to the viability of an organization. The past decade, for example, has witnessed tremendous economic upheavals that have manifested in economic crises, such as the crashes of the Mexican peso, the Russian ruble, and the Brazilian real. Organizational crises have been extensively researched from divergent perspectives, including those of psychology (Halpern 2009), social polity (Weick 2013), and technological structure (Pauchant and Douville 1994).

The organizational crisis literature focuses on myriad factors that influence strategies for crisis management, including the psyche of managers, the nature of crisis-triggering events, organizational structures and processes, and environmental variables (Pearson and Clair 1998). Research on the organizational response, however, has primarily focused on industrial crises (Smith 2010). Industrial crises, such as those related to negative consequences of product consumption (e.g., the silicon breast implants of Dow Coming) and industrial accidents (e.g., the 1984 Union Carbide gas leak incident in Bhopal, India), usually influence a single firm at a time. Research on organizational crises (D'Aveni and MacMillan 2012) shows that surviving firms, in comparison with failing firms, focus on both external and internal environments, which is a critical feature of market orientation (Kohli and Jaworski 2010), and the attainment of a balance between the two environments, which is an important aspect of strategic flexibility (Weaver 1994).

In an ordinary course of events (without a crisis), firms develop capabilities to manage their environment. Organizational investments in these capabilities should reflect the firm's environmental needs (Clark, Varadarajan, and Pride 2004). In environments characterized by high uncertainty, for example, a firm will face many diverse situations and should invest more in being flexible (Harrigan 2012).

The review of crisis and its impact has its roots in a study of risk factors that create vulnerability in organizations. The sociology of risk currently lacks a body of specific systematic knowledge, due to the absence of a consistent base of hypothesis: Weberian sociology, Marxist thought and other theories touch upon but may not completely address the structure of business in an increasingly globalized business environment.

Sound ethics is a necessary precondition of any long-term business enterprise. Businesses should not be torn between doing what's right and what's necessary to make money; in fact, it's bad for business, leading to inefficiency and distrust. A good company fosters and environment that encourages people to develop their values and their skills. Business ethics comprise areas of general principles of duty, rules of conduct, and moral principles (Kleiman, 2014).

Business ethics and social responsibility concern the way a company conducts both internal operations, including the way it treats its work force and the impact that doing its business has on the world around it (Reder, 2014). Companies of all sizes and in all sectors are realizing they function and profit best when they merge their interests with the interests of customers, employees, suppliers, neighbors, investors and other groups affected by their operations (Makower, 2014).

Concerns about eroding standards of business ethics have grown dramatically over the past two decades. A study done at among small business owners demonstrated concern that business ethics be taught as part of a business curriculum in higher education and that ethics should be emphasized more in existing business courses across disciplines. This development occurred at the end of the Reagan administration after emerging insider trading scandals and other questionable business practices. The Reagan administration was notable in having more high-level officials either indicted or convicted than any other administration since President Grant (Gordon, et al., 1985).

Our business system depends on the application of ethical values and the ensuing trust that develops. Superior corporate performance depends on a combination of ethical conduct and shared value systems put into action through a program of internal and external social responsibility (Krikorian, 1984).

The contributions business makes to society are significant. Businesses can confer broad and measurable benefits to the society in which they operate; they can be examples of social responsibility through their day to day operations through pursuit of excellence, competitiveness, innovation and profit. (Hood, 2006).

The private enterprise and free market systems of American capitalism support the growth and expansion of a vital society. Americans are creative and innovative people as a direct result of the free enterprise system allowing for competition and profit. Watson (2012) observes that the operations of the John Deere company, while hugely profitable, served the greater good through the overall social benefit provided by its innovative steel plow that made facilitated prairie agriculture leading to westward expansion. The creation and distribution of goods and services enhance and elevate the overall quality of life; viewing wealth as an evil suggests poverty and privation is inherently better than a life of comfort and plenty. (Watson, 2012)

Mary Parker Follet, considered to be a modern capitalist philosopher, held that great business organizations can only be built when their leaders and administrators identify and align themselves with underlying social impulses of their time, are in accord with stockholder interests, consumer desires, temper of employees and currents of social and business opinion that will shape society in the future (Gabor, 2000).

The professional manager is not an owner disposing of personal property as s/he sees fit, but as a trustee balancing interests of many constituents sometimes conflict (Committee for Economic Development, 2014).

A business's profitability depends upon attaining subgoals including producing a product or service of benefit; employing and retaining skilled knowledgeable employees and encouraging proactive, inspirational management. (Reder, 2014). The value of a corporation goes beyond the tangible assets apparent on a balance sheet and is often mentioned in analyst's review of a company: worker morale, management style, systems for promoting internal innovation, and an ability to predict future trends – all of these abilities and traits of a company weigh into and help determine the expected value of corporate stock. (Hood, 2006).

It is not necessary to use legal or regulatory means to compel all companies to do business in ethically responsible ways. An example is found in the mission statement of Tom's of Maine, reflecting their understanding of the link between profits and a larger accountability: "We believe that the company can be financially successful, environmentally sensitive and socially responsible." (Chappell, 2014)

The discussion of corporate ethics and social responsibility is a continuation of an ancient philosophical debate concerning the morals of commerce itself; even Old Testament books including Deuteronomy layout guidelines for ethical business practices. (Hood, 2006)

However, regarding business and managers as the ultimate responsibility for systemic societal relief, even Plato set limits to the power of rulers in his ideal Republic. To Plato, the greatest injustice would be for members of one class to do the work or heft the responsibilities of another class. More specifically, "the political decisions of guardians should not extend to "contract which different classes of people make in the market". (Warmington and Rouse, ed., 2006)

The issue of the relationship between business and society began in the United States with the Industrial Revolution, though some of its philosophical roots go back further than that.

Utilitarianism, the moral view that the value of a good course of action is evaluated based on what gives the greatest number of people the greatest pleasure or happiness. To the utilitarian, the good person or good company would be a calculating machine making quantitative evaluations what to do based on the greatest benefit to the greatest number of people. The variable in the idea is the subjectivity of the word "good"; in a business whose sole motive is to make money, the "good" is profit; it benefits and the economy benefits. If a business's place in the community, the benefit it may produce by providing work, quality of life, support and more to the people it affects then 'good' may be defined and measured differently. Since a community gives a business infrastructure, services, workers and profits, the business has a responsibility to provide benefits in return. (Chappell, 2014).

Immanuel Kant tried to establish goodness and worthiness as worthwhile in themselves; people should not be treated as a means to some end, but ends in themselves. They should be respected for who they are, not for what they can do for a business (Chappell, 2014).

Milton Friedman criticizes the movement toward corporate social responsibility, calling it 'pure and unadulterated socialism. He writes that profit is the sole purpose of the corporation and its only social responsibility is to engage directly in activities that increase its bottom line, quantifiable profits. His view is that a business entity has no such responsibility, and as long as it 'stays within the rules of the game, that is to say, engages in open and free competition without deception or fraud', it has no other social responsibilities. (Friedman, 1970.)

Most people spend more time on their job than they do on any other single aspect of their lives; it's no wonder, then, that the quality of that experience affects the quality of their lives overall. As Blauner (1964) points out, the nature of a man's work affects his character and his sense of worth and dignity.

In recent years, a combination of factors has led to a paradigm shift related to very basic issues of the nature of work, the workplace, management and employees. The impact of information and communications technology; globalization of markets leading to bigger, more diverse markets and increased competition; and the constant pressure to increase efficiency while reducing costs (Pierce, et al).

Much of the commentry and inquiry into the effect of a job on the worker may be grouped into three categories : the personal goals of the worker ; the social identification the job and the workplace provides ; and the worker's affective feelings on the job.

Sociologists point out that the involvement of the worker in a program or situation that encourages and fosters personal goals helps understand the presence or absence of the alienation which may be characteristic of modern society. Seeman (1959) writes about the issues of 'self estrangement' or the inability of the individual to find actifity that is personally rewarding and fulfilling. It is experienced as monotony, heightened time awareness ('clock watching') and detatchment. The opposite is fond in intérêts and personal involvement ('ownership') in the work and its aspects.

Blauner (1964) points out that due to the social stratification of work (worker/management/executive), the individual may be further dissatisfied due to the inability to see the contribution his own work makes to the larger effort, resulting in the lack of a sense of purpose in his work.

People find personal identiy and a sense of belonging from their social roles : father, mother, manager, member of a church, etc. While family and community are important, work tends to play a central part in the individual's placement in society. It establishes a person's worth quantifiably, in terms of dollars and cents, and has direct bearing on the perceptions of those he most cares about of how well a provider he may be, the type of lifestyle and level of security he can provide his family (D. Miller, 1963).

In the current American society with its increased mobility, traditionally important social groupings have weakened ; ties with larger family groups and with community are less strong than they were fifty or a hundred years ago (Lansing, et al., 1963). Thus, work becomes even more important as a point of identification and personal reference.

Similar to personal goals and social identity are the feelings people experience at work. Employee satisfaction has been of interest to both sociologists and managers for practical problems such as turnover, high absentee rates and patterns in a post-industrial society (Blauner, 1964). Closely associated with satisfaction are the aspects of employee mental health including psychosomatic illnesses, anger, depression and anxiety. These problems are important in terms of their effects on employee quality of life and on costs from illness and inefficiency (Seeman, 1959).

High levels of motivation, a sense of identification with the work and the enterprise, a sense of pride in contribution, and positive social feedback combine to produce employees who are very involved and satisfied with their jobs. These aspects make the job itself more important, more salient and potentially more satisfying to the individual.

Risk refers to future events; therefore, any sutdy of risk is inherently a theoretical activity. Since it is only theoretical, it cannot be directly measured, it can only be projected based on the assumption that future events can be predicted surmised by what has happened in the past, or on observations of the current enviornment and identification of areas of hazard which may cause a crisis and subsequent loss.

Risk is a matter of perspective; every person or business has a selective view of the world, which largely determines which risks or constituents they feel to be worthy of attention; however, perceptions of risk tend to be patterned within cultures, and reflect shared values and beliefs. Every structural arrangement heightens the perceived significance of certain risks while lessening others. Nuclear weapons, war, terrorism, crime and pollution are high on the 'dread list' of contemporary Americans, but every society has its own typical 'risk portfolio' (Douglas and Wildavsky, 1982).

Risk is linked to sociolocial, historical,economic and locational factors. Individuals who share these factors tend to share their exposure to risk. The distribution of what Ralf Dahrendoft calls 'life chances' are not distributed equally throughout society. He discusses life chances in terms of opportunities associated with social living which may cr may not involve a cost or risk exposure, but there is a connection between life chances and risk. (Douglas and Wildausky, P.148)

It is apparent that individuals often have risk imposed on them; at other times, they undertake risk knowingly and willingly for the 'payoffs' they may receive. Risk adverse individuals tend to lead safer and longer lives, but risk tolerant persons tend to be entrepreneurs and others who are successful and high profile in a business community – this high profile and the risk naturally associated with the competitiveness and dynamic factors of any free market society is going to further increase their exposure to the possibility of risk and subsequent crisis. The risk in any situation can be viewed on a relative scale from voluntary to involuntary: a person can voluntarily go sky diving for the payback of the adrenaline rush, but the adrenaline rush that motivated survivors down the stairs at the World Trade Center was not induced by events of their choosing (Dahrendorf, 1979).

Max Weber used his observation of the complexity of business and of living to point out that, historically, traditional and modern, communal and rational, communist and captialist elecments emerge in ever new combinations (Roth, 1978).

For Marx, the distribution of risk is a matter of social structure. Further, he states that man is human *because* he is social; and that while the first historical act was to procude the means to satisfy one's baisc needs, production was the beginning of people's social relation. Marx states that people distinguish themselves from other animals by their production of the means of their subsistence. The process of production creates organization and the worldview appropriate to it; productive activity becomes productive relations. He states, (people)

'...produce only by cooperating in a certain way and mutually exchanging their activities. In order to produce, they enter into definite connections and relations with one another, and only within these scial connections and relations does their action on nature, does production take place.' (Giddens, 1973).

The web of social relations, according to Marx, is the essence of human activity by which people continually create and change the world. Social structure is continually being created and evolving out of the activities of individuals as they live, work and play, but especially as they produce materially. He felt that true human freedom rests on man's association and dependence upon others in these areas.

The further back we look at history, the clearer it becomes that the producing individual has always been part of a larger whole. Stages of production have certain common benchmarks and common purposes which can only be accomplished through cooperation.

Risks multiply as technology expends, as wars multiply, as we invade more of nature and create organizations that increae risks for the operators, passengers, innocent by-standers and for future generations. Many risky enterprises have catastrophic potential, to take the lives of hundreds of people out in a moment, or to shorten or criple the lives of thousands more. Human-caused catastrophes appear to have increased with industrialization and every day the potential for devices to crash, sin, burn or explode increases as well. We are haunted dialy by risks of varying probability, magnitude and emotive impact : dioxin in the air, thrihaolmethanes in the drinking water, pesticides in food, drunken drivers on the highways, nuclear power plants or nuclear waste depositories in our backyards, and overriding all, especially at the start of a new millenium the double whammy of the threat of extinction through war and terrorist acts coupled with the fear of economic crisis.

The good news is that by understanding the risks we may be able to reduce or even eliminate some of the dangers inherent in contemporary life and in doing business.

The public reception of how a business deals with a risk and its various factors of 'fallout' will depend on cultural ideas about justice and ethics. It is often held that perception of risk and crisis handling is directed by issues of fairness. The more that organizations depend on personal commitment rather than coercion for issues such as employee performance and loyalty, consumer brand recognition and loyalty, and supplier commitment to timely and economical cooperation, the more exlicitly they are monitored for fairness. The threshold of acceptability in the workplace is lowered when constituents consider themselves ignored or exploited.

However, the concept of fairness allows for cultural, economic and social variations of perception of individuals or interrelated organizations having different 'stakes' in a company's handling of a crisis situation. Selsnick found that fairness means one thing to unskilled manual workers (fairness being equal treatment for all), and another to clerical, professional and management groups (fairness as fari recognition of individual ability). Therefore, it is highly possible that despite a firm's best intentions to maintain operations and minimize the impact of a crisis on those companies and individuals affected, how well, completely or responsibly that may be done is ultimately vulnerable to a highly subjective review by each and every one of those constituents (Selsnick, 1969).

The subject of business ethics is complex. Fair-minded people sometimes have significant differences of opnion regarding what constitutes ethical behavior and how ethical decisions should be made. The following are four accepted approchwes that business owners and corporate exeutives can use to consider ethical questions. Even with these guidelines, the method chosen may not suit everyone involved, but by rational consideration of alternatives, it is possible to make decisions that are consistent with the mission statement of the organization.

1. **Utilitarian** the utilitarian approach to ethical decision making focuses on taking the action that will result in the greatest good for the greatest number of people. For example, if a business owner had to choose whether to lay off workers in an effort to downsize after a crisis, or to relocate operations to utilize lower wage foreign workers in a less-regulated market, that company might result in retention of market share, enabling the company to pay the remaining employees the same or higher wages. However, if a company refuses to consider such an option, it may be unable to remain competitive. This could result in layofs of the U.S. workers whose jobs produce essential income. On the other hand, moving operations and using low wage workers may tend to depress the wages of the workers in the entire

industry, thus reducing almost everyone's standard of living and depressing their ability to purchase the same goods the company and others are trying to sell.

2. **Moral Rights** The moral rights approach concerns itself with moral principles, regardless of the consequnces. Under this philosophy, some actions are considered to be right or wrong; if paying low wages is immoral, a company's deisre to stay competitive and survive is not a sufficient justification to do so. In the extreme, the company should close down if it cannot be operated by paying workers a 'living wage', rgardless of the actions of competitors or survival of the business.

3. **Universalism** The universalist approach to ethical decision making is similar to the Golden Rule. This approach has two steps: first, a determination is made as to whether a particular action should apply to all people under all circumstances. Next, it is determined whether the individual in charge of the decision would be willing to have the action applied to themselves. Under this approach, a company would detemin if paying extremely low wages in response to crisis and competion would be right for the company and for everyone else. If so, then it would be followed with consideration if someone would be justified in paying the decision maker those low wages if s/he, as a worker, had no alternative except starvation.

4. **Cost-Benefit** Under the cost-benefit approach, the costs and benefits of taking versus not taking a particular action are lanced against one another. For example, one of the costs of moving operations overseas to take advantages of extremely low wages might involve negative publicity. That would be weighed against the competitive advantage that might be gained by taking that action.

In a complex and dynmaic global business climate, ethical decision making is rarely easy and is rarely black and white. Sometimes one of the above approaches will be appropriate, sometimes another will be the right way to approach and ethical evaluation. When time is taken and full consideration is givien, then businesspeople are more likely to make a decision that later turns out to have been ethically correct.

Social justice combines the three principles of needs, deserts and equity; however, at certain points, each comes into conflict with the others. Human needs are set by social standards; deserts accord rightful compensation and consideration to the well-deserving, and equity in business depends on the size of the affected interest as well as the resulting effect crisis will have on that person or entity. This means, for example, that a loyal supplier that has dedicated a large part of their capital and means of production to a company experiencing a threat to business continuity is deserving of consideration, especially if that dedication put at risk the business survival of that supplier.

Businesses develop continuity plans focusing on their own mission critical components; it is appropriate and ethical that they view this procedure as including other entities affected by crisis as well. A business impact analysis takes this process further and provides greater detail. It examines business process composition and priorities, dependencies, cycles, and service levels, and, most important, the business process dependency on channels of supply, distribution and operations. The requirements for a business impact analysis generally fall into four categories: (1) business process composition, execution cycles, and support; (2) operational priorities, service levels, dependencies, and relationships; (3) the primary and collateral business risk and the business scope of their impact; and (4) the costs and benefits of business continuity strategies and alternatives. Each area has detailed information requirements that are essential to providing effective business continuity. For example, the analysis of business process support should provide information on the technical, functional, organizational, and infrastructure support requirements. When collected, analyzed, and synthesized, the information defines a model of critical processes and risks to the business. These tools provide consistent analytical structure and processes, and help to standardize the impact analyses throughout the enterprise. Core business processes and supporting business areas include both manual and manual and automated functional requirements, manual and automated system support requirements, infrastructure support requirements, suppliers, customers, service levels, processing cycles, and the external and internal business drivers.

Charles Fried attempted to develop a moral and ethical theory of group exposure to risk in his book, *Anatomy of Values*. He theorizes that an individual or entity participates in a common risk pool into which each 'dips' when operations expose others to dangers. Any society operates its rules of mutual accountability, judgment and retribution from the principle of whether then individual exposes others unduly to risk without accepting responsibility for the outcome that may ensue. It suggests the duscussion of a risk management plan should include addressing the social, economic and human risk along with the assessment of the physical probabilities of risk. Therefore, instead of concentrating on how much risk is acceptable to a company and how its own profitability and continuity may be maintained, the wider and more generally responsible question would be what kind of a business environment does one want to create?

Expectations that a rational individual or responsible entity will act in a moral way is part of the American sense of jutice and is a separate but salient cultural dimiension of doing business, implying a heirarch of moral and ethical values adoped by rational businesspersons to enhance a vibrant business environment and economy they are working to build and from which they expect to ultimately benefit.

Opposing Views: In his article "The Social Responsibility of Business is to Increase It's Profits, Milton Friedman criticizes the movement toward corporate social responsibility, calling it 'pure and unadulterated socialism. He writes that profit is the sole purpose of the corporation and its only social responsibility is to engage directly in activities that increase its bottom line, quantifiable profits. His view is that a business entity has no social responsibility towards any constituency other than its owners and investors, and as long as it 'stays within the rules of the game, that is to say, engages in open and free competition without deception or fraud', it has no other social or ethical responsibilities. In short, his position is that since a corporation is not a person; it has no responsibilities.

To understand Friedman's position, it is necessary to understand where he comes from. A Nobel Prize winner for Economics, Mr. Friedman is widely regarded as the leader of the Chicago School of Monetary Economics, which stresses the importance of the quantity of money as an instrument of government policy and as a determinant of business cycles and inflation. He follows the Keynesian view that the road to a healthy economy is paved with policies of more spending and lower taxes. He has also been a key advisor to conservative Republicans who tend to promote the laissez-faire concept of dealing with business.

Therefore, it would follow that he would reject the idea that business had any responsibility to contribute anything further than jobs and business for the supply chain and product/service distribution outlets. Finance 101 students chant daily: "The job of the Finance Officer is to maximize the value of the stock." Friedman leads that chant, stating unequivocally that the manager is an employee of the owners of the business, and his key, and only, responsibility is to them.

Friedman sees the imperative of social responsibility as a threat to the bottom line – that any monies not specifically spent on the product/service and consequently reflected in profits is a violation of the trust a company's owners place in its managers and employees. He feels that stockholders or customers or employees could spend their own money on social initiatives should they wish to do so. He feels that social responsibility is another form of taxation – or, taking money from the entity that made that money and redistributing it to the public at large. This, he persuasively argues, is not social responsibility, but socialism. Since the business has already been forced to pay taxes, the political mechanism should distribute that money and then leave the corporations alone.

Friedman refers to Adam Smith that expectations should not be placed on businesses that only know and care about business. He says that those who push for "social responsibility" do so because they cannot accomplish their aims through political means; that pressure on business people to do other than what is strictly their business circumvents the political process of fair representation.

Perhaps Friedman sells businesses and managers short when he says they should only be expected to understand profits and the operation of a business. If a manager is an employee of a company, it is not only his job to maximize profits, but to run the company consistent with the goals of the owners which may (and probably do) reach beyond dollar profits. Businesses typically develop a business plan as a map to keep on the right heading toward their goals – an integral part of a business plan is a mission statement. The mission statement defines the overriding 'mission' of the company, or what it is in business to do. It describes the nature of the business, the specific market, and the constituency. It is no accident that business plans include their communities and employees as constituents to whom they have a responsibility. The business plan of Tom's of Maine is: "We believe that the company can be financially successful, environmentally sensitive and socially responsible."

Business success derives from a synergy of inputs, including the work of employees who are skilled and knowledgeable, a management team that understands how to inspire competent and motivated performance through sensitive and responsive management of a continually changing workplace.

Mr. Friedman is an economist – he deals with equations and theories, and that is all very well and good. However, business does not operate in a vacuum – it affects and is affected by its environment – and to a point, Mr. Friedman agrees, stating that the peripheral good created by the commerce provided by a successful company is all the benefit it should be required to provide to a society and its community. If he were a businessperson he would understand that "goodwill" is carried as a quantifiable value on the accountant's books because it is an asset built up through an investment of time, commitment and money. Business people know that people will do business with people they like or they feel good about being associated with; a company that is blindly pursuing profits does not generate a positive entry in the 'goodwill' category.

It cannot be argued that a company enjoys the safety and security to operate in an environment provided by police, national defense, transportation infrastructure and many other benefits provided by general funds. It seems only pragmatic that those who enjoy the benefits should pay for their implementation. Friedman may dislike taxation and management responsible and sensitive to the needs of its interrelated constituency of customers, employees, suppliers and more, and he may feel that responsible management may drain funds and valuable time from direct use within a business, but it is clear that it would be difficult to function without the indirect benefits of the participation of those constituents.

A study reported in Rosabeth Kanter's book, The Change Masters asked human resources experts which companies were most progressive in their industries; it was found that the more progressive companies were more profitable and fostered greater growth over 20 years than did their counterparts.

Friedman states the doctrine of social responsibility is a cloak for actions justified on other grounds. He feels that calling expenses that improve communities and quality of life is morally wrong – that if it is being done to indirectly benefit the company, it should be stated outright because to do otherwise simply enforces the idea that business is wicked and the pursuit of profits is bad.

It is not the cloaking of intention that is morally wrong, it is the blind pursuit of profits oblivious to the whole picture of the corporate environment – recognizing the benefit of the inputs of a healthy society as well as the benefits received by support of that society. Just like breathing, oxygen supports the body; exhalation returns carbon dioxide to the atmosphere; plants use it to make more oxygen.

Embracing corporate social responsibility is not just the right thing to do, it is key to developing a work and social environment that directly and indirectly contributes to a company's competitiveness and survival.

Increasing technology, which has fostered an era of business globalization introduces both new ethical questions and review of the structure of the business environment. Now as never before, elements of risk are linked with social and political structures.

Social and business structure study must pay attention to the interdependencies in social relations and transaction. Conceptions of how these interdependencies work together must consider both action and order. The structure of the business community involves both the autonomous actions of any individual company as well as the actions of whole industries.

As suggested by Douglas and Wildausky (1982), the concept of a social structure has three basic aspects:

1. the units or parts that comprise the whole and their characteristics relative to one another;
2. the relationships that join the parts to form a larger configuration and the characteristics of those relationships and;
3. the parameters that separate and enclose the parts to form the larger whole.

Interaction networks involve the actual interaction of actors who occupy positions in relationship to one another. The relationships, the types of transactions and social exchanges and the flow of agreements, contracts and information are all ways of characterizing the relationships in a social or business structure.

An example is in the building of a house: the carpenters, plumbers, masons and electricians interact with each other as well as with the managers and developer to form a network, which is the basic unit of structure to get things done. Multigroup systems, such as business organizations, involve corporate officials, office workers, maintenance personnel and others also have similar observable connections to each other in the interactive process. It is the web of group affiliation, the manner in which associations are formed and transactions made that causes all involved to be mutually exposed (to a greater or lesser degree) to the any crisis affecting any of the others.

The problem of understanding how the structure is ordered in the business environment involves determining how the decisions of constituents (investors, employees, suppliers, and customers) and even competitors are shaped and maintained by the ongoing business of mutually dependent companies.

CHAPTER 3

Risk Management

During times of crisis it is very important for a responsible organization to be able to management risk. Risk management is one of the most difficult and challenging tasks facing business and industrialized nations today. Doing just about any type of business involves a degree of exposure to the possibility of loss, from mild to extreme. Any business at any time may be exposed to many types of loss, or in turn, expose those having contact with or affected by the business to a potential loss. For example, most hazardous technologies confer benefits on society in the form of better health, increased productivity and an overall higher quality of life, and yet may expose workers and nearby residents to chemicals introduced into the air or water supply.

Successful businesses take calculated risks to achieve objectives. Globalization, deregulation, Web-based services, complicated financial instruments and contracts, emerging markets--all contain tremendous potential advantages for companies and carry the danger of huge mistakes or unexpected developments. Businesses must measure these risks, try to minimize them and--if possible--use them to their advantage.

Business risk can be defined as "a concept used by managers to express concern about the probable material effects of an uncertain environment on business goals." Risk is only a conceptual device that helps us to deal with the consequences arising from our inability to predict the future with certainty. Managers put assets at risk to achieve objectives, whether the organization is for-profit, not-for-profit, or governmental. The task of management is to achieve these objectives in an uncertain environment; thus, management becomes synonymous with risk management. This focus on goals distinguishes business risk from other risk concepts (McNamee, 2000).

A socially and ethically acceptable risk management strategy has to balance the exuberance and openness of doing business in a open society and free market economy with the due care and diligence to ensure not only ongoing operations of any specific business but that of interrelated aspects of the respective industry and the larger economy.

The balancing process is controversial because both risks and benefits are often intangible and there is no general agreement on the way they should be valued. In the absence of measurable statistics and definite knowledge, opinions tend to be colored by factors including but not limited to: personal values, what the public and business community are sensitive to at a particular time, and professional judgment, leading to different assessments of the relative significance of particular risks. In the effort to manage risks, public and private authorities must mediate not only amongst competing economic and political interests, but also amongst conflicting technical interpretations based on widely divergent views from different sources with their own agendas.

All of the assets and constituents at risk in the organization should be addressed by a comprehensive risk management plan, including: financial assets, such as cash, credit and negotiable instruments; physical assets, such as land, buildings and equipment; intangible assets, such as brand, reputation and information; and human assets, such as knowledge, skills and the commitment and contributions of the people involved without whom the organization would not be able to function or maintain its unique identity.

Some risks are ignored and others receive considerable attention and scrutiny. Current social arrangements, particularly power relationships and the role of the mass media, are influential. According to Mary Douglas, a prominent sociologist, political and economic reticence to address ethical risk management policies is not a sign of lack of perception, but rather of the intention to protect certain values and their 'accompanying institutional forms. However, her research indicates that people take the threat of natural disasters more calmly, and with less sense of injustice and less desire for retribution than when they believe they are victims of man-made disasters. This is salient to our discussion as business leaders address their management programs in terms of the responsibility of their organization to the interests of its constituents (Bodein, Pugliese & Anthony, 2011).

The most effective management of risk exposure takes into account that life is uncertain; that in the course of competitive effort, changing markets, political unrest, globalization and industry conditions, business becomes riskier. Through an ongoing process of identification and awareness, policies and procedures are reviewed and established to proactively plan for possible management of a variety of crisis scenarios. In this manner, given the event of a loss or accident, costs in terms of operational limitations, financial outlay and personal effects are minimized and planned for, providing for minimum disruption and expense.

The purpose of a risk management program is to integrate awareness, safety and efficiency into the system of operations to minimize the possibility of loss and mitigate losses that may occur. Through this manner, a company may increase the probability of meeting its income and operational projections, maximizing it's the credibility of overall management and subsequently, overall share value.

Implementing a risk management program may involve some initial costs, but the benefits in the long run outweigh the additional overhead. While even the safest program cannot predict and avoid all crises or losses, proactive Risk Management can provide ways in which potential crises, risks and constituents who may be affected adversely by a crisis situation can be identified, and consequently, effective alternatives and safeguards put into place.

Disaster preparedness planning allows for the ability to influence overall losses that manifest through interruptions in revenue, loss of tangible assets and loss of human resource assets by taking a proactive stance towards planning and implementation of risk management principles. A risk management program fosters the overall mission of the organization through its pre and post loss objectives. Optimally, this will be done at the least cost to the organization consistent with statutory and OSHA regulations. A risk management program helps increase site safety, secure a reduction in insurance costs, and improve production and distribution capabilities through increased efficiency and effectiveness in a safe and sustainable manner.

This can be done by working within the existing system, enhancing the management framework already in place to achieve the organization's objectives. A goal of a comprehensive risk management program is to provide the oversight and methods of cooperation between discrete organizational units to generate a synergy. With cooperation from management and staff, it is possible to effectively identify exposures, examine the most feasible means to deal with the risks they impose, select the best risk management techniques, implement our decision and monitor the results. Everyone who works in or for the company should beware, understand, and follow the risk management program for their safety and benefit and the benefit of the entire organization and extended constituents.

In case of loss, the most basic need is to plan for and insure the survival of the organization from an operational standpoint - that its productive integrity remains intact. Continuity of operations without interruption is another key goal, including ongoing profitability, stability of earnings, and ultimately maintaining goals for growth.

When a loss happens, operations can become disrupted, there is cost of cleanup and repair, loss of income to workers, a change in the insurance experience rating resulting in higher premiums, a loss of reputation and goodwill, and numerous other effects, both quantifiable and intangible. Dealing with these occurrences is the negative side of Risk Management. On the other hand, while risk management's major thrust is to minimize the effects of accidental loss on an organization, it can also have dramatic overall effects on seemingly unrelated areas. These effects include enhancement of marketing results due to increased customer goodwill and company reputation; higher comfort level of management to take on increased opportunity and increased profit; the security of a safe workplace environment for workers; and the raising of finance from investors assured of a far-sighted and flexible management of the organization.

CHAPTER 4

Risk Management and Business Ethics

A responsible risk management program is integral to doing business in an ethical manner. The exposure to risk affects not only a company's survival and profitability, but the survival and quality of lives of many other businesses and individuals the company may touch in the course of operations. An ethical risk management program considers all the impacts of a potential loss, from the standpoint of all constituents, then plans for an provides responsible management and recovery options.

A structured, logical program uniquely appropriate for a company is the foundation of a successful risk management effort. The best way to implement an effective risk management program is through the participation and support of everyone in every department.

Through an efficient and effective program it is possible to provide benefits to the organization that will far outweigh the costs of setting up and implementing the program.

A business's profitability depends upon attaining subgoals including producing a product or service of benefit; employing and retaining skilled knowledgeable employees and encouraging proactive, inspirational management. The value of a corporation goes beyond the tangible assets apparent on a balance sheet and are often mentioned in analysts' review of a company: worker morale, management style, systems for promoting internal innovation, an ability to predict future trends – all of these abilities and traits of a company weigh into and help determine the expected value of corporate stock.

A thorough understanding of the business process requires a collaborative approach. Organizations doing ethical and practical crisis planning need a concept or organizing principle across departmental lines, that can assist them to plan, design and undertake a thorough reordering of the ways in which they conduct every aspect of their business, starting with what they input from suppliers and ending with what they output into the environment.

Each risk group is a collection of specific business risks, some of which are common to all organizations, and some that are industry-specific. Examples of common specific risks include those associated with dysfunctional workplaces, such as harassment, theft, sabotage, injury, employee lawsuits, and violence. Industry-specific risks differ for banking, public-sector agencies, and manufacturing, for example, depending upon the nature of their markets, the extent of government regulation, their customer or constituent segment, the nature of their technology and its rate of change, and other external threats.

Acquiring an understanding of business risk is linked to at least three elements: a thorough understanding of the business process, imaginative tactics for generating ideas about possible effects of risks, and a framework or risk model that provides a common language for discussing risk. Brainstorming sessions, self-assessment workshops, templates, and checklist tools are among the common devices that can stimulate thinking and ideating about the risks within an organization and the individuals and businesses connected to the business via channels of responsibility whose interests must be ethically addressed.

Most people have an intuitive understanding of risk based on their common sense and experience, but it may be this very common-sense approach that lulls them into false comfort. Obvious risks are no real threat, given a reasonably alert management. Instead, it is "unintended consequences" that challenge our common sense and experience.

Categories of risk: Risk can be categorized by the areas of management it most directly affects and which would be responsible for any losses incurred.

Ownership risks include but are not limited to the following:

- External threats: Forces outside the control of the organization that can affect the organization's business processes and goals. Examples include customer or constituent demands; labor, financial, and product markets; suppliers, including unions; competitors; government regulation; economic and political forces; technology; and physical and environmental forces.

- Custodial risks are associated with owning and safeguarding assets. Examples of custodial risks include obsolescence, damage in handling or storing the assets, and theft from storage.
- Hazards, which are shared with process risks, are related to loss or impairment through fire and other natural or man-made disasters and accidental loss.
- Opportunity costs, which are shared with behavioral risks, represent the cost of making less-than-optimum decisions about asset acquisition and disposition. Examples include purchasing the wrong asset, paying too much, selling the asset too soon or too late, selling the asset too cheaply, and disposing of the wrong asset.

Process or Operational Risks are those to which the operations of the business expose the organization and those connected with it to various vulnerabilities. These include but are not limited to:

- Hazards, which are shared with ownership risks, are associated with loss or impairment through fire and natural or man-made disasters and accidental loss.
- Errors, omissions, and delays represent the risks to processes arising from random differences in human or machine activity in the process. Examples of these risks include but are not limited to poor judgment in plans or operations, inappropriate or outdated control mechanisms, and machine malfunction.
- Frauds can arise from intentional misrepresentation of suppliers, employees, and customers. Examples of these risks to the process include theft, bid rigging, bribery, kick-back schemes, and customer abuse.
- Productivity loss, which is shared with behavioral risks, can result from poor design of the process or its control system. Examples include scheduling conflicts, inappropriate work rules, missing controls, lack of monitoring control systems, underutilizing assets in the process, and goal conflicts.

Behavioral risks are those associated with personnel and management exposures including:

- Productivity loss, which is shared with process risks, arises from poor management practices or poor worker commitment. Underutilizing human assets, poor leadership, favoritism, lack of work structure and discipline, inconsistent management decisions, and personal and work goal conflicts are examples of these risks.
- Dysfunctional workplaces can represent risks to employees who work in a dysfunctional environment and risks to the organization because employees are working in such an environment. Examples of these risks are gender or racial harassment, excessive pressure to meet objectives without compensating relief valves, employee theft and sabotage, workplace injuries, employee lawsuits, and workplace violence.
- Opportunity costs, which are shared with ownership risks, are associated with the cost of making less-than-optimum decisions about the acquisition and disposition of human assets--people, knowledge, and skills. Hiring the wrong people, a poor compensation system, and letting the wrong people or skills leave the organization are prime examples.

It may sound like a lot of exposure and a lot of bad news, especially to managers or staff not trained in the creativity of proactive "what if?" scenarios; but beneficially, the flip side of Risk Management is the opportunity that can be realized from the process. Suddenly whole new ways of thinking about production processes, energy usage, packaging, product design, raw materials and even ownership become apparent. In most cases, the soundest and most ethical way of doing things from a risk management point of view, turns out to make economic sense as well. Most methods of safe, managed production concurrently increase business efficiency and efficiency means saving labor, time, energy, materials and money, often all at once.

Some specific benefits of effective Risk Management include:

- Avoiding the costs of fines, cleanups and litigation.
- Reducing the amount of capital assets lost or threatened.

- Reducing the amount and costs of energy.
- Reducing the costs of waste handling and disposal.
- Creating an atmosphere that fosters confidence in development of new products and services for new market opportunities.
- Having greater credibility with banks and other financial institutions.
- Maintaining eligibility for less expensive insurance.
- Reducing risks of major environmental disasters.
- Developing and importing new technology.
- Improving the organization's public image.

The benefits of Risk Management come down to a basic idea: sustainable performance leading to minimizing expenses and maximizing profits through management of assets, maintenance of cash flow through secure, safe and sound operational procedures.

Risk management can succeed only when it works within the context of a company's environment, goals, objectives and strategies. Organizations may differ greatly in their risk tolerance and management styles, and therefore it is impossible to order up a one-size fits all risk management program.

The potential of a disaster or smaller loss must be considered in the context of the environment in which a business operates. Once a company understands the risks of an undertaking, the owners or management can develop a strategy for containing them. This may involve formally structured policies and procedures or an informal process, depending on the business. Companies may bring in risk management consultants, such as CPAs, to help the business get to this stage. As part of the risk management process, company leaders might ask the following questions to pinpoint the operational and ethical issues that must be addressed:

- What are our goals and objectives?
- What are our values?
- Who is accountable?
- Who has the authority?

Questions like these can help establish the context for an organization's ethical handling of risk management. Once these larger areas have been established, a process of micro-examination covers the various aspects of a company's operations, facility, staff and other facts of the organization to identify possible risk exposure. While this can be tedious, it is important for a full and responsible plan to be established. Whether done in-house or by a third party professional Risk Manager, ethics and business consideration require development of a risk identification system that's rigorous, flexible and pertinent to a company "under the microscope".

Judgment and ethics come into play in determining the extent to which planning is done. To an extent, it is good for people to know exactly what they will do in a crisis; but on the other hand, each situation is different and it's not possible to predict what any person or group of person involved will bring to that situation. From an ethical standpoint, the severity of an event dictates response: a life-threatening situation calls for a different focus than one in which there is a danger of loss to property. A company would be expected to get people out of a burning building before being concerned about losses to machines and equipment; and every convenience store clerk is always trained to immediately turn cash over to an armed robber – money and tangibles can be replaced, human life cannot. Physical exposures, which include obvious and catastrophic risk from political, natural or other disasters, there are other aspects and categories of operations involving exposure that would cause a ripple effect to a business' constituents due to a fluctuation or interruption in profitable, ongoing business operations. Lesser-known but equally devastating risks might be product quality risk, reflecting quality control problems; regulatory risk resulting from political changes affecting an organization's industry, market or environment; cultural risk, which is damage to a company's product, brand or corporate image due to changing attitudes or perceptions on the part of customers; and trade war risk, which is an intra-industry crisis occurring when price gouging or other anti-competitive practices are experienced.

Once a company has exhaustively examined the possible risks to which it is exposed, it is then necessary to rank the risks according to factors such as the impact a loss or crisis from each risk would have on ongoing operations, profitability, and the place a business occupies in the web of interrelationships that makes up its industry, market and economy.

A profitability crisis can be both a business and an ethical problem, ACT International, a U.K.-based financial software maker, made specific operational choices to detect and mitigate risk. From an initial period of rapid growth, it moved into a slump in which business and profits plummeted in the early 1990s. A customer survey clearly showed the company had failed to recognize profound customer unhappiness with its products and support. The company solved the problem, in part, with a program to elicit ongoing customer feedback. During the profitability crisis, however, the company was forced to layoff workers, cutback on production, reduce orders from suppliers and dividends to stockholders. They had responsibility, both ethically and financially, to these constituents to manage the crisis, identify and rectify the problem and reduce the risk on an ongoing basis (Bodein, Pugliese and Anthony, 2011).

The ethics of how a business fits into this web of interrelationships and the ripple effect of a crisis was evident in the recent events concerning Enron. Enron is a major company, based in Houston, Texas, providing energy throughout the world. For many years, they have been a leader in development of power plants and related infrastructure projects in countries from those which are highly industrialized and developed, such as the United States, to those classified as 'emerging'. Their extensive development projects required billions of dollars, necessitating extensive borrowing and creative financing. Through mishandling of funds and resources, combined with SEC reporting deliberately concealing private interests and internal problems, Enron came under governmental scrutiny, its stock plummeted and the company declared bankruptcy. These events represent a wide combination of risks, including credit risk (inability to pay back monies borrowed), fraud risk (misrepresentation to almost all constituents of the company), cultural risk, brand equity risk, and many more. These risks can easily be characterized as ethical and business exposures.

The result of Enron's situation is that thousands of stockholders lost money, employees lost pensions invested in the stock, projects stand idled causing unemployment all over the world, Enron's own employees are out of work – ever widening ripples affecting the worldwide economy due to Enron's ethical risk exposure.

It is an interesting point that Enron's fall may have significantly touched the lives of as many people and operations of contingent businesses as the damage caused by two planes flying into the World Trade Center. These are examples of how different categories of exposure can result in losses equally devastating to the public, each in their own way. While Enron represents catastrophic losses caused by an ethical and monetary crisis, the World Trade Center losses came from political and physical damage risks.

Could a proactive Risk Management program have prevented either crisis? With the benefit of hindsight, it's easy to guess but impossible ascertain. Perhaps either crisis could not have been prevented, but the severity of the loss might have been significantly mitigated if procedures had been in place to monitor and check on Enron's accounting, or if plans had been made to evacuate the World Trade Tower's more quickly and through other options.

This is not to condemn the Risk Management procedures of those responsible for either situation; as stated previously, risk management relies heavily on predictions and "what if?" scenarios predicated upon past events. Currently, high rise owners are arranging contingency plans in the event of terrorist attacks and architects are planning buildings able to withstand the high heat generated by an explosion, but the expectation of due care is limited to what might reasonably be expected to occur. Other than Hollywood screenwriters, who might have had the imagination to pre-construe the events of September 11th? Ethical risk management, then, is concerned with both prevention and mitigation, resulting in plans to manage a crisis as well as its aftermath.

Quantitative data can play an important role in identifying situations with risk implications. A less well-known and less extreme example is Canadian Pacific, a diversified operating company involved in transportation, energy and hotels. Its bottom line and contingent business contacts are is affected by external factors, such as fluctuations in the prices of crude oil, natural gas and coal, as well as movements in interest and foreign exchange rates. These factors indicate that the company could be vulnerable from exposures inherent in country risk, political risk, regulatory risk, currency risk, fraud risk, catastrophic risk and more. This is the kind of quantitative analysis that Risk Managers consider to help clients or employers assess threats and opportunities though thoughtful "what if?" situations (Bodein, Pugliese and Anthony, 2011).

To increase the chances of achieving objectives and providing ethical response and proactive prevention/mitigation, Risk Managers can help employers or clients establish and monitor critical success factors and key performance indicators, which signal whether a strategy is working or failing.

Once identified and established, an ethical Risk Management program should be implemented and integrated with daily operations, as well as in relationships with suppliers, distributors, employees and other constituents. An infrastructure for risk management includes the reporting and operational policies to include the entire organization, not just the Risk Management department. It is vital to include all employees from management to administration to operations – those dealing with problems and situations on a daily basis are best able to recognize a risky or potential crisis situation, so channels of communication and solicitation of participation is vital to the success of any program.

Ongoing feedback should be elicited to make sure that management has identified the exposures and that appropriate risk strategies are in place, including awareness and communications training for employees. Ongoing management, monitoring and feedback helps to create a culture in which employees and others become personally and voluntarily accountable for ongoing management of risk to avoid or mitigate potential crisis situations.

Contingency Planning - The first and most important aspect of any contingency plan provides for communication. If a disaster hits our plant, where do we go? What do we do? How do we protect ourselves, our employees and our assets? Typically this first level of reaction is covered by basic compliance with OSHA and industry regulations which require precautionary measures such as adequate fire extinguishers, hoses, first aid kits, fire drills, building evacuation plans and much more. A certain amount of communication before the fact is needed so that people know what to do in an emergency, how to protect the equipment and themselves, where to go to be counted, what to do next, where to get more information. After the fact, ongoing communication with stockholders, employees, the media and suppliers is necessary. How do we protect the plant and resume operations as soon as possible?

A contingency plan is part of a good risk management program. Have you ever tried to frustrate an ant by dropping a leaf or rock in front of him when he's on his way somewhere? First he tries to go around one way; if you block that way, he'll try the other, and if you block that way, he'll go over the top of the (what may be to him a significant) obstacle. That's the mindset needed to survive a disaster at a plant. Planning and flexibility allow for the preparedness level of having other ways to go, other ways to do things. These may be provided by redundant operations, by shifting production to other plants, by getting repair people in as fast as possible to keep machinery and people working with as little downtime as possible.

The September 11 attack set up a situation unprecedented in American business: air traffic, which carries a significant amount of cargo and information between companies and companies and between companies and customers, was completely halted for almost a week. Not only that, but New York City, a major business area, was completely blockaded; its access blocked while law enforcement tried to bottle up any terrorists or evidence to keep them from getting away. This is a nightmare of supply chain logistics no one could have envisioned prior to that date.

It is important to establish primary, secondary and even tertiary suppliers and means of distribution. If air shipping is not available, we must be able to ship by train; if not by train, then by truck. How, who, when and what are not journalistic questions but the nuts and bolts behind making multiple contingencies viable.

Planning is the first step and goes hand in hand with security. Terrorism is not a new threat, it just seems to be hitting home right now. Although we have armed and trained security persons on patrol at all times, each employee becomes a security officer in a special way: each employee is (or should be) completely aware of what is normal for their particular area of the plant. Each employee should be alert to changes or irregularities and report them to management and/or security right away. A loose package, suspicious and unusual powder or substance, something not where it should be or a situation or setup that looks "odd" or "funny" can be much more than a coincidence.

It is more important than ever that employees know who and what belongs here and what doesn't. Could that be a lunchsack left behind or a bomb? Could that powder be coffee creamer or a dangerous substance placed there to harm or disable our employees? There has been a lot of coverage of "scares" and "hoaxes" and some of them seem silly – point is: they are funny and silly and stupid until one, just one, is real. We need to maintain an open door policy to encourage awareness, while not cultivating an atmosphere of undue fear and suspicion.

Dealing with the conflicting issues of making people feel secure while maintaining vigilance will be a challenge facing all risk management professionals now and in the foreseeable future. Never before has it been so true that you if you fail to plan, you're planning to fail.

Awareness is the best preventative and proactive stance: crisis situations usually evolve, but if they are caught during their evolution, the chances of being able to responsibly contain adverse affects are highly increased. Most crisis situations have 'leading indicators' – something in the environment that warns of an impending situation – a mind set incorporating awareness is important in proactive crisis and risk management. The question "what if?" should be constantly on the minds of any effective manager. In most cases, attempts to manage a situation occur too late – during or after a crisis when prevention is no longer possible and 'damage control' is being done during a stressful time. Most people are accustomed to making decisions under normal conditions, but by definition, nothing about a crisis is 'normal', - managers attempting to run an ongoing company effectively, efficiently and profitably and do damage control at the same time are bound to produce less than optimal decision-making. This can result in a situation in which decision making can actually be counterproductive to the main goals.

The immediate task is to define the 'critical issue'; then determine the list of constituents to solicit their support, define critical operations (risk management) and ultimate goals.

Any team in charge of handling a crisis must be small, capable of moving quickly and the authority and credibility of making decisions. The crisis team must have members that are functionally diverse to provide a multi-faced point of view. It is a basic tenant of organizational behavior studies that there are two *de facto* organizations in any company: the formal and the informal. The formal is depicted on the organizational chart while the informal organization consists of those individuals who really make things happen.

In a recent example of crisis management, as soon as the Boesky indictment hit, Drexell Burnham Lambert organized to handle the crisis, forming a crisis team, or 'War Council' as it became known. On the team were top members of management: president, chief finance officer, chief legal counsel, vice president of marketing, vice president of government affairs and internal and external PR staff. Daily meetings allowed all individuals to be updated as to what was happening in events and response in the rest of the organization, and how to handle the unraveling crisis while focusing on action plans to keep business going as usual.

Effective goals are to keep the business going and strong, while maintaining positive public opinion towards the organization, maintain morale, and minimize impact on the business.

CHAPTER 5

Ethical Marketing
– Post-9/11 Considerations

Marketing after a crisis becomes less an issue of what an organization would like to do than a problem of how to do it sensitively, appropriately and ethically. A major issue facing marketers and advertisers since the September 11 terrorist attacks is what do they sell and how do they sell it in a changed world. Advertising and marketing were happening in relation to a major public event, the "War on Terror", the "All Anthrax All the Time" news networks, a recession, and the largest increase in unemployment in five years.

Consumer attitudes and options have always driven the creative talents of marketers and advertisers; the way they live and perceive the world affects how products are positioned and marketed, so it's important that they know what people are thinking and how they can communicate effectively with them.

The following themes keep cropping up throughout the media and are reflected in current advertising campaigns: returning to the family, making work meaningful, enjoying small rituals, aspiring to simplification, moving spirituality forward and recognizing the sanctity of life. These all reflect basic desires for stability and a sense of purpose in life. They show that people are thinking "bigger picture": they aren't as fascinated by trivial matters but are looking inward and to their own close circle of family and friends. In this type of world, crass external intrusions will be vehemently rejected. Advertisers are recognizing this, toning down their messages and appealing to what can be called "core values" – they have learned to get to the point and concentrate on the immediate benefits to the consumer's quality of life and comfort.

Whether it's "patriotism" or "fear" marketing, what it comes down to is a question of taste and ethical restraint. Advertisers were scrutinized against benchmarks of ethics and taste more closely and critically than ever. Were companies and marketers selling goods and services in an appropriate manner, given the national climate? Or, were they capitalizing on sentiments they should not? Were they creating demand or feeding the demand created by the news media?

With the media saturated with messages about anthrax, Afghanistan and terrorism, consumers were being bombarded by many conflicting messages advertisers cannot ignore; yet, even with how sentimental people became about returning to core values of family, religion and patriotism, they are sensitive to the fact that those sentiments can be used and abused by marketers to manipulate consumers. Therefore marketers have to recognize that at a certain point, a saturation level is reached and messages come across as just another crass attempt to make a buck. While consumers are primed to do the right thing in response to demands they be patriotic and spend their money, they're extremely sensitive to ad taste. There's a very fine line between being appropriately patriotic and disgustingly opportunistic.

It seemed as though every company rushed to their ad agencies demanding broadcast of their contribution to the relief efforts and also to "pull" ads that might be deemed insensitive in the days following September 11. Others including American Express and General Electric put out general messages of condolences and support, highlighted heroes and heroic actions in their spots, and family became a recurrent theme in selling products.

It's interesting to see the reactions of people and how they respond to messages; while older consumers can get weepy at images of the flag, younger people may be unaccustomed to patriotic themes in an age of globalization.

Overall, the message is to provide images and concepts that give people a little peace of mind during trying times. People are also seeking increased personal control. While the world seems to be spinning out of control, and geopolitical forces are affecting the lives of ordinary citizens, people are looking to have greater influence over what they can control as a way of bolstering themselves against that which they can't.

Companies with their pulse on the public, including Gallup and other major pollsters predicted people were going to start to look at ways to relieve the pressure of an anticipated long "war" and the time needed to come back from recession, not to mention the strain of the holidays so soon after the shock of the World Trade Center attacks. Marketers were advised to focusing on escapist entertainment and comfortable "cocooning" to get away (temporarily) from news and business pressures. Consumers were wary of appeals to conspicuous consumption but could appreciate small indulgences and marketers were advised to incorporate escape themes into advertisements for vehicles, music, games and even Las Vegas has promoted its gambling venues in this manner.

This doesn't mean that consumers want to ignore tragic events; actually something inside them resonates with the lost heroes and they were looking for a way to make a personal heroic stand. The message from the White House and government is that regaining normalcy is a way of fighting back, and marketers who wanted to reach the public correspondingly emphasized the heritage and longevity of their brands. "New" isn't a good attribute in a time when change is overwhelming and threatening. Instead, stability can help consumers assure themselves that some things are rock solid and can be relied upon.

In this climate, where foundations, stability and normalcy are the overriding focus, any attempts to indulge in ostentatious spending, make minute distinctions between equivalent brands or even to adopt a healthier "new" lifestyle, could turn consumers off in droves. The climate has been reminiscent of when the Gulf War dampened travel and other business activity, sent consumer confidence crashing and caused companies to put advertising and innovations off to a more 'upbeat' time.

The tone has changed, as marketers abandon frivolous appeals to self-indulgence and focus on family, community and other enduring values. Ads are also less "funny", as marketers are hesitant to expose themselves to criticisms for taking what may seem to be a crass attitude. There is nothing funny or creative about thousands of people dying – and a jovial or irreverent commercial thirty or sixty second spot in the middle of tragic news could or would provide a jolt to the sensibilities that might backfire in the face of the company that spent so much for that time and that advertising. "Kinder and gentler" would be two salient adjectives for ads at this time.

Just as the public is fearful, so are companies. The immediate impact of the WTC attacks was extensive and expensive: retail shutdowns, cancelled sporting events, postponed conferences. Many companies have decided to hold off on advertising at this time, or to tone down advertising they currently have booked – there is a fear of taking risks, while at the same time pushing for the American way of life and expressing faith in the ultimate recovery of the economy.

The airlines have suffered the worst. They were already in difficult financial shape before the attacks, but since that time, the fear and increased difficulty of flying continues to depress the travel industry. The attacks also caused both United Airlines and American to change their ad campaigns; United to spots with a more "upbeat" tone, and American introduced a fare sale called "The Great American Get-Together" and promoted the extension of double frequent flyer miles. This may not be sufficient to overcome people's fear of flying and increased hassle.

Companies have generally slashed advertising spending during tough times, and these tough times are no different. CFO.com reports that spending will be down 6 percent in 2001 from the previous year (Frieswick, 2001). However, conventional wisdom is that a recession or tough times is a wonderful time to build business and reputation. In addition to traditional marketing channels, leading companies can invest in low-cost channels such as e-mail marketing. Those that survive and live to sell another day will be those that invest in customer relationship management and focus on that toward high returns and lasting ongoing loyalty.

The Wall Street Journal reported on December 10, 2001 that there is actually quite a bit of money in the hands of consumers at this time; however they are unsure exactly what to do with it. Having seen huge losses in tech stocks, they are hesitant to invest in the stock market, which sorely needs it; yet, many have refinanced their homes and other big-ticket items to the new lower rates afforded by cuts Greenspan and Company have made in the prime lending rates. But is buying really a patriotic act, as the government and marketers would have us believe? Should people go to shows, buy computers, cars, more and more Christmas toys to show they're good Americans? Will that work?

History is not supportive of a positive result: Japan tried it and it didn't work. The Japanese government issued checks to people and said "buy" in order to stimulate their flagging economy. They didn't.

In the wake of terrorism and during the war, advertisers and marketers are putting on a "brave face" – trying to encourage both companies and consumers to spend – consumers on products and services, and companies on their advertising budgets. Only time will tell if things get back to 'normal' – whatever that is. However, it is clear that after the crisis, the newly-righteous public will be sensitive to any apparent breech of ethics or taste, or any similar exploitation of the situation in presenting advertising or marketing.

CHAPTER 6

Discussion, Analysis and Conclusions

A responsible business that plans to be around for a long time must have a plan for when a crisis occurs. No two crises are alike; they are typically unanticipated and evolve quickly, even if they have leading indicators to warn of the impending occurrence. Advance planning is essential, because once underway, a crisis takes on a life of its own and is constantly changing as various constituent interests are affected. The response the affected organization makes to evens often triggers reaction by others who must also be addressed as part of an ongoing crisis management and control effort.

A highly effective strategy is to have a crisis team ready to act and make decisions quickly and with authority. Each member of the team has pre-planned and designated responsibilities and should be aware of the overriding mission of the company, the potential for peripheral entities to be affected and maintain a high state of awareness for control of what may be an escalating, expanding situation.

Numerous factors need to be anticipated and assessed to provide for the optimal response from operational, loss control, profitability and ethical standpoints. Companies that deal successfully and ethically with a crisis always try to anticipate the next possible thing that could happen and take control of the situation proactively. Companies that are reactive or that try to minimize damage through inactivity inevitably prolong the crisis.

In the midst of a crisis, it is important that crisis team members resolve to keep a sense of perspective and objectivity, otherwise thoughts of the potential impact and the threat to the company and constituents could provide a significant distraction that could negatively impact the effectiveness of the control efforts.

No matter the company or government entity, an organization is continually operating in a "crisis environment" – the potential for a crisis, or event having significant impact to an organization and its constituents is always present and proactive planning for this possibility should be viewed as a fundamental business requirement. Advance planning can minimize the damaging impact of a crisis; how much or how little an organization prepares, and the thoughtfulness and ethics of how that planning is done will shape the organizations response.

It is important to assess how management has dealt with emergencies in the past to gain an indicator of possible ways to improve reaction in the future.

From an ethical stand point, it is important to determine how all the organization's constituents will be affect by potential crisis developments, how a company plans to communicate, direct, handle and work with these groups during a crisis. These constituents include but are not limited to employees, dealers, distributors, customers, consumer interest groups, stockholders, the media, industry experts, competitors and government officials and regulators.

Actual plans of action for response to potential crisis situations should be developed and reviewed on a regular basis to reflect the company's growth, development, changing situations and environment so that the strategy remains comprehensive and viable.

When a crisis occurs, the organization must instantly size up who is involved, the human emotions involved and how ethical handling of these aspects will influence how response is made. Crisis are rarely diffused by facts, they are diffused by how the organizations involved deal with them and how people subsequently feel about how well that was done. The effective crisis team will stay sensitive to the emotional and ethical needs of various constituencies. Too often, companies that are in process of maintaining operations will forget about how a crisis impacts constituent's financial status or security - if the business does survive, it will need the support of constituents, and it is ethical to support them in anticipation of that mutual dependency.

A company's ability to deal with a crisis successfully is dependent upon the ability of management to be honest and ethical with itself and its constituents and to remain factual and realistic. That attitude would have helped Exxon minimize the negative publicity generated by the Valdez oil spill in Alaska- a slow response to the media, insensitive answers to questions and apparent lack of concern for the citizens and environment of Alaska resulted in extremely negative media coverage and enraged consumer and environmental groups. Thousands of customers returned their Exxon credit cards. Worse, the positive steps Exxon took later to pay for and manage cleanup were obscured by initial insensitivity and lack of ethical handling and consideration of constituent groups and interests.

The Exxon Valdez and more recently the BP Oil spill that took place in the Gulf of Mexico crisis occurred at a time when U.S. consumers were increasingly sensitive to environmental issues; however, both Exxon and BP Amoco officials failed to take that into account, reacting as though the oil slick was 'no big deal' and that they had no responsibility for the environment or damaged habitat for waterfowl and fish. Advertising and marketing at the time of a crisis must be sensitive to the situation and appropriate. While some organizations prefer to suspend these activities until after the smoke clears, others realize that advertising and marketing can play a supporting role in rallying public support and maintaining a company's place in the market during a crisis.

The long-term legal concerns of a company impacts how it reacts and proceeds in a crisis; in general, counsel will want to protect the company from lawsuits, reduce its long-term liabilities and protect it from any implication of wrongdoing either in conjunction with the occurrence of the crisis or its cleanup. Therefore legal counsel will tend to advise toward the least amount of information and contact with outside or contingent persons as possible. Conversely, marketing and public relations personnel tend to focus on corporate image, sales, and immediate impact of the crisis. Management must take responsibility for weighing short-term and long-term objectives and balancing the public's perception with potential liabilities.

Ultimately, every crisis comes to an end, or at least subsides to the point where normal operations may be resumed. Oddly enough, resumption of day to day life involves a total letdown, emotionally.

Crisis work is typically intense and all-consuming, moving quickly in many directions that the calm after the storm can be severe.

If crisis members experience such a letdown, they can always remember that crisis probability is a constant in an increasingly competitive, risk-rife society, and that another crisis may be just around the corner, ready to challenge the plans and experience that have been developed proactively to keep the business and the constituents viable and ongoing business entities.

REFERENCES

Aaker, David A. and Briance Mascarenhas (2014), "The Need for Strategic Flexibility," Journal of Business Strategy, 5 (Fall), 74-82.

Abolafia, Mitchel Y. and Martin Kilduff (2008), "Enacting Market Crisis: The Social Construction of a Speculative Bubble," Administrative Science Quarterly, 33 (2), 177-93.

Achrol, Ravi S. and Philip Kotler (2009), "Marketing in the Network Economy," Journal of Marketing, 63 (Special Issue), 146-63.

Allen, Linda and Christos Pantzalis (2013), "Valuation of Operating Flexibility of Multinational Corporations," Journal of International Business Studies, 27 (4), 633-53.

Ansoff, H. Igor (2012), "Strategic Issue Management," Strategic Management Journal, 1 (April/June), 132-48.

Arthur, W. Brian (2009), "Competing Technologies, Increasing Returns, and Lock-In by Historical Events," The Economic Journal, 99 (March), 116-31.

Axelrod, R. (1984). The evolution of cooperation. New York: Basic Books.

Badaracco, Joseph L., Jr., and Richard R. Ellsworth. (2009). *Leadership and the Quest for Integrity*. Boston: Harvard Business School Press.

Baljko, Samuel & Scott, Dennis (2009) "Hoping During Stringent

Economic Times". The Wall Street Journal, Dow Jones & Company, Inc., pp. 34-37 Oct. 23

Blauner, David.(1964) The Importance of Finding the Right Job:

Keys to Becoming a Better Man. Forest Press.

Brownell, Eileen O. (1999) The Magic of a Positive Attitude. Baby Shop Magazine, Available: http://www.spindlepub.com/babyshop/fall99/bsf997.htm.

Bodein, Tarbaush & Pugliese, Mayor & Anthony, Sidney. Tips and Techniques to Responsible Business Practices. Univ. of Utah Press. (2011)

Carbone, James. (2009) "Supply Chain Management gets outsourced". Purchasing, February 11.

Chappell, Tom. (2014). *The Soul of a Business*, New York: Bantam Books.

Clark, Terry, P. Rajan Varadarajan, and William M. Pride (2004), "Environmental Management: The Construct and Research Propositions" Journal of Business Research, 29 (1), 23-38.

Committee for Economic Development. (2014). *Social Responsibilities of Business Corporations*. New York.

Copacino, William C. (2008). "Masters of the Supply Chain". Logistics Management and Distribution Report, December 31, v32, i12 p.23(1)

Crum, Susan. (2010). "Contract Manufacturers are Managing Growth at Every Level". Changers Business Information, February.

Cryer, Bruce A. (1996). "Neutralizing Workplace Stress: The Physiology of Human Performance and Organizational Effectiveness". Presented at Psychological Disabilities in the Workplace Seminar, The Center for Professional Learning, Toronto, Canada, June 12, 1996.

Cyert, Maryl and March, Robert. (1963). "Doing Business During Tuff Times". William Morrow & Company

D'Aveni, Richard A. and Ian C. MacMillan (2012), "Crisis and the Content of Managerial Communications: A Study of the Focus of Attention of Top Managers in Surviving and Failing Firms" Administrative Science Quarterly, 35 (December), 634-57.

Diba, Ahmad. (2000). "Blessed are the Piece Makers", Fortune, May 1.

Dingle, D.T.; Spruell, S.P.; King, A and Hocker, C. (2001). "Bouncing Back". Black Enterprise, December. Vol 32, Issue 5, p. 77-83.

Douglas, Marcus & Wildausky, Lucy. (1982) The Threat of Nuclear Weapons During Times of War. Conari Press.

Evans, Stuart J. (2011), "Strategic Flexibility for High Technology Maneuvers: A Conceptual Framework," Journal of Management Studies, 28 (January), 69-89.

Federal Benchmarking Consortium. (2007). Serving the American Public. Washington: National Partnership for Reinventing Government.

Fink, Steven. (2001). Steven Fink's Study of Fortune 500 CEOs

Fried, Charles (1982). Anatomy of Values

Friedman, Milton. (1970). "The Social Responsibility of Business is to Increase Its Profits", New York Times Magazine.

Frieswick, Bryan. (2001). Tech. Companies Slashing Advertising Expenses. Financial Times. Sept. 17

Gabor, Andrea. (2000). The Capitalist Philosophers, New York: Random House, Inc.,

Gordon, Peter J., Charles R. Wiles and Judith A. Wiles. (1985). *"A Study of the Ethics of Small Business Managers"*. Southeast Missouri State University

Giddens, Anthony. (1973). Capitalism and Modern Social Theory; An Analysis of the Writings of Marx, Durkheim and Max Weber. Cambridge Univ. Press

Gottschalk, Marie. (2013) Appropriate Code of Conduct for Small Business. Cornell University Press.

Gutek, Barbara A. (2005). The Dynamics of Service. San Francisco: Jossey-Bass Publishers.

Gutek, Barbara A. (1999). The Social Psychology of Service Interactions. Journal of Social Issues, Fall.

Hachman, Mark. (2000). "Components Shortage Squeezing Profits out of the Supply Chain". Electronic Buyers' News, May 29.

Halpern, C.F. (2009), "Cognitive Factors Influencing Decision Making in Highly Reliable Organization," Industrial Crisis Quarterly, 3 (2), 143-58.

Harrigan, Kathryn Rudie (2012), "The Effect of Exit Barriers UponStrategic Flexibility" Strategic Management Journal, 1 (2), 165-76.

Harvey, Tom. "Service Quality: The Culprit and the Cure." Bank Marketing, 1 June 1995 volume 27(number 6): p. 24. Hawken, Paul. (1993). "A Declaration of Sustainability", *Utne Reader*

Hebard, Clifford C. "A Story of Real Change." Training & Development, 1 July 1998, volume 52(number 7): p. 47+.

Hinkin, Timothy Robert. "How to Treat High-Achieving Managers." Journal Of Retail Banking, Fall 1991, volume 13(number 3): p. 38+.

Ho, Rodney. (2000). "SCI's Profit, Revenue Won't Meet Forecasts", Wall Street Journal, September 14, 2000.

Hood, John M. (2006). *The Heroic Enterprise: Business and the Common Good*, New York: The Free Press

HR Zone. (2001). "Job Stress: An Overview – Something Every Manager, Supervisor and Employee Needs to Know." HR Zone Magazine Online.

HR Zone. (2001) Job Stress: An Overview. Something Every Manager, Supervisor and Employee Needs to Know. HR Zone, 3.

Industry Week. (1998) P.42-46. Nov. 2

Jaljko, Jennifer L. and Ismini Scott. 2009). "Build-to-order Model Getting First Real Test". Electronic Buyers' News, October 25.

Jaworski, Bernard J. and Ajay K. Kohli (1993), "Market Orientation: Antecedents and Consequences," Journal of Marketing, 57 (July), 53-70

Kanter Rosabeth. (1976) The Change Masters

Kinlaw, Dennis C. (1993). *Competitive and Green: Sustainable Performance in the Environmental Age*, San Diego: Pfeiffer & Company.

Kleiman, Carol. (2014)."Adding Ethics to Family/Work Considerations". *The Chicago Tribune*

Kohli, Ajay K. and Bernard J. Jaworski (2010) "Market Orientation: The Construct, Research Propositions, and Managerial Implications," Journal of Marketing, 54 (April), 1-18.

Kostanturos, John. "Embracing the Discomfort of Change." U.S. Banker, 1 February 1996, volume 106(number 2): p. 73+.

Krikorian, Robert V. (1984). "Ethical Conduct and the Bottom Line", an address before the Tax Executive Institute Tri-State Tax conference, Milwaukee, Wisconsin

Kwong, Jo Ann. (1988). "Corporate Donors Embrace Free Market Environmentalism", *The Wall Street Journal*

Lewis, Robert C. and Richard E. Chambers. (1989). Marketing Leadership in Hospitality. New York: Van Nostrand Reinhold.

Lyndenberg/Marlin/Stub. (1986). "Rating America's Corporate Conscience". *Council on Economic Priorities.*

Makower, Joel. (2013). *The E Factor: The Bottom Line Approach to Environmentally Responsible Business.* New York: Times Books.

Makower, Joel. (2014) *Beyond the Bottom Line: Putting Social Responsibility to Work for Your Business and the World.* New York: Simon and Schuster.

McNamee, Raymond (2000) "Managing Effective Risk Management in the 21st Century". Ohio State Univ. Press.

Naj, Amal Kumar. (1988). "See No Evil: Can $100 Billion have 'No Material Effect' on Balance Sheets?", *The Wall Street Journal*, Dow Jones & Company, Inc., pp. 1 and 11.

O'Dea, Ann. "The human touch." Bank Marketing International, 1 December 1998: p. 9-10.

Orr, Ginger. (2000). Hospital Takes System of Stress Management to Heart. Chicago Tribune, March 16.

Pauchant, Thierry and R. Douville (1994), "Recent Research in Crisis Management: A Study of 24 Authors' Publications from 1986 to 1991," Industrial and Environmental Crisis Quarterly, 7 (1), 43-61.

Pearson, Christine M. and Judith A. Clair (2008), "Reframing Crisis Management," Academy of Management Review, 23 (January), 59-76.

Pierce, J.L., et al. (1989). Alternative Work Schedules. Boston: Allyn and Bacon, Inc.

Plastiras, James. (1999) Human resources industry faces various changes." *Capital District Business Review (Albany)*, 21 June, posted on line 21 June 1999, viewed at URL [http://www.bizjournals.com/albany/stories/1999/06/21/focus1.html}. Viewed on 8 January 2001.

Reder, Alan. (2014). *In Pursuit of Principle and Profit*, New York: G.P. Putnam's Sons.

Sagawa, Shirley, Eli Segal, Rosabeth Moss Kanter. (1999). *Common Interest, Common Good: Creating Value Through Business and Social Sector Partnerships*, New York: Simon and Schuster.

Self, John T. (1998). "Are You Stressing Out Your employees? Creating a Supportive Environment". Improving Customer Service, 16.

Seeman, Ronald. (1959). "Building Character by Finding the Right Job. Oliver Books.

Serant, Claire, (2000). "Japan Begins Opening Doors to North American CMS", E-Business News, July 3.

Smith, Denis (2010), "Beyond Contingency Planning: Towards a Model of Crisis Management," Industrial Crisis Quarterly, 4 (4), 640-57.

Solomon, Robert. (1999) *A Better Way to Think About Business: How Personal Integrity Leads to Corporate Success*. New York: Prentice Hall.

Reuters Magazine (1999) P.23. Nov. 8

Roth, Charles. (1978) Max Weber and Postmodern Theory : Rationalisation Versus Re-Enchantment. Florida State Univ. Press.

Teeter, Deborah J. and G. Gregory Lozier, ed. (2006). Pursuit of Quality in Higher Education: Case Studies in Total Quality Management. San Francisco: Jossey-Bass Publishers.

Warmington, Eric H. and Philip G. Rouse, editors, *Great Dialogues of Plato: The Republic*, Book IV, p. 289.

Watson, Charles E. (2012). "The Meaning of Service in Business", *Business Horizons*

Weaver, Henry Grady. (1984). *The Mainspring of Human Progress.* New York: Foundation for Economic Education, 1984

Weick, Karl E. (2013), "Enacted Sensemaking in Crisis Situations," Journal of Management Studies, 25 (July), 305-17.

Whiteley, R. & Hessan D. (2006). Customer Centered Growth: Five Strategies for Building Competitive Advantage. Boston: Addison-Wesley Publishing Company.